OF THE CROSS

PRAYING THE STATIONS

ALFRED MCBRIDE, O.PRAEM.

ST. ANTHONY MESSENGER PRESS
Cincinnati, Ohio

RESCRIPT
In accord with the Code of Canon Law, I hereby grant my permission to publish
The Challenge of the Cross: Praying the Stations, by Alfred McBride, O. Praem.

Most Reverend Joseph R. Binzer
Auxiliary Bishop
Vicar General
Archdiocese of Cincinnati
Cincinnati, Ohio
September 2, 2011

The permission to publish is a declaration that a book or pamphlet is considered
to be free from doctrinal or moral error. It is not implied that those who
have granted the permission to publish agree with the contents, opinions or
statements expressed.

Scripture passages have been taken from *New Revised Standard Version Bible,*
copyright ©1989 by the Division of Christian Education of the National
Council of the Churches of Christ in the U.S.A., and used by permission.
All rights reserved.

Cover and book design by Mark Sullivan
Cover and interior illustrations courtesy of Gene Plaisted | The Crosiers

LIBRARY OF CONGRESS CATALOGING-IN-PUBLICATION DATA
McBride, Alfred.
The challenge of the cross : praying the stations / Alfred McBride.
p. cm.
Includes bibliographical references and index.
ISBN 978-1-61636-303-1 (alk. paper)
1. Stations of the Cross. 2. Catholic Church—Prayers and devotions. I. Title.
BX2040.M347 2012
232.96—dc23
2011036645

ISBN 978-1-61636-303-1

Published by St. Anthony Messenger Press
28 W. Liberty St.
Cincinnati, OH 45202
www.AmericanCatholic.org
www.SAMPBooks.org

Printed in the United States of America.
Printed on acid-free paper.

12 13 14 15 16   5 4 3 2 1

INTRODUCTION

As I move into my later years, I am attracted more than ever to the Stations of the Cross.

Perhaps it's because Christ spent his last moments on earth publicly bearing all kinds of physical pain—beatings, bleeding, weakness, and a series of humiliations—and because I have witnessed (and paid more attention to) suffering of all kinds in more recent years.

Perhaps it's also because Jesus moves me to accept the various slings and arrows of life, not hiding them, rather publicly living my own version of the cross in union with my Lord. In so doing I feel much closer to Jesus in his Passion and am humbled by his courage and love. I am more aware of the salvation he won for me.

I know now more than ever that praying the Stations of the Cross can lead me to a treasure of graces and spiritual growth.

FOLLOW THE PASSION OF CHRIST

The Stations of the Cross, or Way of the Cross, is a devotional practice that follows the Passion of Christ from his condemnation before Pilate to his death on the cross and his burial. Originally these stations were developed in Jerusalem and had great appeal for the pilgrims to the Holy Land as early as the fourth century. Pilgrims processed from one site in the Holy Land (a "station") to the next site, and at each site expressed their faith in hymns, prayers, and silence as a way of remembering and being part of Christ's own way of the cross.

In the Middle Ages the Franciscans spread throughout the church this devotion that an English pilgrim, William Wey, in 1428 first named "Stations of the Cross." The Holy See had already attached an indulgence to this pilgrimage, and later the indulgence was given to those who could not travel to Jerusalem but did so in spirit back home.

Many monasteries and retreat centers created outdoor stations after the Jerusalem model. Eventually, most churches and chapels mounted fourteen images of these scenes on their walls, with images ranging from pictorial representations to abstract symbols. For private devotion, people walked from station to station. For public devotion a priest, accompanied by servers and someone leading with a crucifix, processed through the church from station to station while the congregation followed the prayers and hymns from their pews.

In recent times, a fifteenth station, "Jesus Rises from the Dead," has often been added so that the full reality of Christ's saving work in his death and resurrection is celebrated. On Good Friday 1991, Pope John Paul II celebrated an alternative to the traditional stations that reflects more deeply on the scriptural accounts of Christ's Passion, as seen in the following comparison:

TRADITIONAL STATIONS

1. Jesus Is Condemned to Death
2. Jesus Takes His Cross
3. Jesus Falls the First Time
4. Jesus Meets His Mother
5. Simon of Cyrene Helps Jesus
6. Veronica Wipes Jesus' Face
7. Jesus Falls Again
8. Jesus Speaks to the Daughters of Jerusalem
9. Jesus Falls the Third Time
10. Jesus Is Stripped of His Clothing
11. Jesus Is Nailed to the Cross
12. Jesus Dies on the Cross
13. Jesus Is Taken Down from the Cross
14. Jesus Is Laid in the Tomb
15. Jesus Rises from the Dead

POPE JOHN PAUL II'S STATIONS

1. Jesus in the Garden of Gethsemane
2. Jesus, Betrayed by Judas, Is Arrested
3. Jesus Is Condemned by the Sanhedrin
4. Jesus Is Denied by Peter
5. Jesus Is Judged by Pilate
6. Jesus Is Scourged and Crowned with Thorns
7. Jesus Bears the Cross
8. Jesus Is Helped by Simon the Cyrenian to Carry the Cross
9. Jesus Meets the Women of Jerusalem
10. Jesus Is Crucified
11. Jesus Promises His Kingdom to the Good Thief
12. Jesus Speaks to His Mother and the Disciple
13. Jesus Dies on the Cross
14. Jesus Is Placed in the Tomb

For *The Challenge of the Cross*, we will follow the traditional stations and add the fifteenth station, "Jesus Rises from the Dead."

HOW TO PRAY THE STATIONS

The Stations of the Cross, one of the church's oldest and most durable forms of popular piety or devotion, extends the liturgical life of the people but does not replace it. Devotions such as the rosary and slow, prayerful reading of Scripture are time-honored ways to rouse and enrich our faith and open us to a stronger commitment to the sacraments and the Liturgy of the Hours.

The Challenge of the Cross is ideal for lenten devotions at parish churches or by other groups wishing to pray together. I also recommend that *The Challenge of the Cross* become a regular addition to a person's private devotion at home, during long commutes, or in assisted living, nursing care, or hospice situations. While Lent is a common time to pray the Stations of the Cross, we can find much inspiration from the devotion throughout the year.

Each of the fifteen stations in *The Challenge of the Cross* includes a Reflection that focuses on Jesus' thoughts and acts in his Passion and that helps you apply a station to your own life. Station themes include references to everyday life experiences, such as caregiving; making rash judgments; facing pain and death; dealing with disappointments, losses, and betrayals; finding discipline for the life journey; recognizing the need to forgive and be forgiven, and so on. Following each Reflection, you will find a Scripture to Ponder, a Prayer to Meet the Challenge of the Cross, and a Closing Prayer.

In a congregational setting, the leader can open the devotion by announcing each station and saying, "We adore you, O Christ, and we praise you," to which the group then responds, "For by your holy cross, you have redeemed the world." The leader and the group read aloud the two-part reflection, followed by the leader or another reader saying, "Let us pray to meet the challenge of the cross." The group can together recite the Scripture to Ponder. The leader or another reader then begins the petition, with the group responding. Each station ends with all reciting the Closing Prayer.

To enhance the devotion, whether in a church or private setting, each station could open with a hymn from any available hymnal. Typically this could be the English version of the "Stabat Mater," whose words can be found on page 9. The "Stabat Mater" is a thirteenth-century hymn to Mary that meditates on her suffering during the crucifixion of her son, Jesus. The song would be ideal to begin or end each Station of the Cross.

LINK YOUR CROSS TO CHRIST'S PASSION

As you pray and follow these Stations of the Cross, I hope you will recognize and experience the link between your particular crosses and Christ's Passion and see the purpose Jesus had in living and dying among us. There is no love without sacrifice.

I hope you will receive this gift from Christ, who in the darkness of the cross already glimpsed the rising sun of Easter.

Stabat Mater

At the Cross her station keeping,
stood the mournful Mother weeping,
close to her son to the last.

Through her heart, His sorrow sharing,
all His bitter anguish bearing,
now at length the sword has passed.

O how sad and sore distressed
was that Mother, highly blest,
of the sole-begotten One.

Christ above in torment hangs,
she beneath beholds the pangs
of her dying glorious Son.

Is there one who would not weep,
whelmed in miseries so deep,
Christ's dear Mother to behold?

Can the human heart refrain
from partaking in her pain,
in that Mother's pain untold?

For the sins of His own nation,
She saw Jesus wracked with torment,
All with scourges rent:

She beheld her tender Child,
Saw Him hang in desolation,
Till His spirit forth He sent.

O thou Mother! fount of love!
Touch my spirit from above,
make my heart with thine accord:

Make me feel as thou hast felt;
make my soul to glow and melt
with the love of Christ my Lord.

Holy Mother! Pierce me through,
in my heart each wound renew
of my Savior crucified:

Let me share with thee His pain,
who for all my sins was slain,
who for me in torments died.

Let me mingle tears with thee,
mourning Him who mourned for me,
all the days that I may live:

By the Cross with thee to stay,
there with thee to weep and pray,
is all I ask of thee to give.

Virgin of all virgins blest!
Listen to my fond request:
Let me share thy grief divine;

Let me, to my latest breath,
in my body bear the death
of that dying Son of thine.

Wounded with His every wound,
steep my soul till it hath swooned,
in His very Blood away;

Be to me, O Virgin, nigh,
lest in flames I burn and die,
in His awful Judgment Day.

Christ, when Thou shalt call me hence,
by Thy Mother my defense,
by Thy Cross my victory;

While my body here decays,
may my soul Thy goodness praise,
Safe in Paradise with Thee.

   —translation in *Lyra Catholica* by Edward Caswall,
1849

Leader: We adore you, O Christ, and we praise you.

All: For by your holy cross, you have redeemed the world.

REFLECTION

Leader: In the court of the high priest, the assembly judged that Jesus was guilty of blasphemy and he deserved to die: "They spat on him, and took the reed and struck him on the head" (Matthew 27:30). In the court of Pilate, the Roman ruler perversely sought to save Jesus by having him beaten and crowned with thorns. Pilate thought that it would stir sympathy, but it didn't. Then Pilate gave the people a choice between the innocent Jesus and Barabbas, a convicted murderer. The people chose the guilty one, and Pilate followed the popular will—not what he knew was right. Our creed memorializes his moral failure to save Jesus in the words "suffered under Pontius Pilate."

All: When I look at the unfair judgments endured by Jesus for our salvation, I think of the judgments I have made in my lifetime. I mistreat innocent people and sometimes, sadly, those closest to me. I rush to judgment when patience is needed. Even my own relationship with Jesus is sometimes marred by unjust thoughts. I also have been hurt by false judgments made against me. I have survived, but I always need moral and spiritual purifications. Standing beside Jesus when he bore my sinfulness in silence, I experience a mix of regrets and a power flowing from him into my soul.

SCRIPTURE TO PONDER

All: Answer me when I call, O God of my right!

You gave me room when I was in distress.
Be gracious to me, and hear my prayer. (Psalm 4:1)

PRAYER TO MEET THE CHALLENGE OF THE CROSS

Leader: Let us pray to meet the challenge of the cross.

All: Lord, curb my tendency to rush to judgments. Jesus, help me bear with patience the times when I will be unfairly treated.

Leader: Let us respond to each petition with "Lord, hear my prayer."

- For the grace of repentance and conversion, I pray, *"Lord, hear my prayer."*

- For wisdom in dealing with disagreements, I pray, *"Lord, hear my prayer."*
- For courage in witnessing my faith, I pray, *"Lord, hear my prayer."*
- For help for the persecuted church, I pray, *"Lord, hear my prayer."*

CLOSING PRAYER

All: Jesus, often I still judge others too quickly despite what I have learned in my life experience. I can still be unwilling to consider the needs and motivations of others. I excuse myself too easily. Forgive me, Lord. Amen.

JESUS TAKES HIS CROSS

Leader: We adore you, O Christ, and we praise you.

All: For by your holy cross, you have redeemed the world.

REFLECTION

Leader: Jesus often spoke of the cross. In effect he said, "If any want to become my followers, let them deny themselves and take up their cross and follow me" (Matthew 16:24). What he preached, he practiced. St. Paul writes: "He humbled himself / and became obedient to the point of death— / even death on a cross" (Philippians 2:8). St. Paul often preached the cross, as he does again to the Corinthians: "When I came to you, brothers and sisters, I did not come proclaiming the mystery of God to you in lofty words or wisdom. For I decided to know nothing among you except Jesus Christ, and him crucified" (1 Corinthians 2:1–2). And before St. Paul, Isaiah prophesied the meaning of Christ's cross: "He was wounded for our transgressions, / crushed for our iniquities; / … by his bruises we are healed" (Isaiah 53:5).

All: I have lived long enough to know that everyone has known physical, emotional, and spiritual pain. It is unavoidable. I like St. Paul's advice about our crosses: "I appeal to you…to present your bodies as a living sacrifice, holy and acceptable to God" (Romans 12:1). Facing my pain, disappointments, losses, betrayals, dreams unattained, I need to live my own version of Christ's Passion. St. Paul says, "I have learned the secret of being well-fed and of going hungry, of having plenty and of being in need. I can do all things through him who strengthens me" (Philippians 4:12–13). I do not suffer alone. Jesus is with me in those who stand by my side, my sickbed, my embarrassment, my office, my parish, my home.

SCRIPTURE TO PONDER

All: In my distress I called upon the LORD;
    to my God I cried for help.
From his temple he heard my voice,
    and my cry to him reached his ears. (Psalm 18:6)

PRAYER TO MEET THE CHALLENGE OF THE CROSS

Leader: Let us pray to meet the challenge of the cross.
All: Lord, show me how to share in your cross by

deeper repentance. Jesus, give me the humility I need to carry my cross.

Leader: Let us respond to each petition with "Lord, hear my prayer."

- In the disappointments, trials, and pain we all face, I pray, *"Lord, hear my prayer."*
- For all who face serious illness and for those who care for the sick, I pray, *"Lord, hear my prayer."*
- For the poor, the neglected, and forgotten, I pray, *"Lord, hear my prayer."*
- For those near death, I pray, *"Lord, hear my prayer."*

CLOSING PRAYER

All: I pray for everyone who is facing pain so that each person may come to realize the redemptive value of suffering by union with Christ's Passion. I pray for all Christians who suffer for their faith in Christ. May I never forget that there are still martyrs for Jesus today. May the frustrations I experience be balanced by the comfort I receive from Christ, whose graces sustain me. May I share with those in distress the comfort I have known through my relationship with Christ. Amen.

Leader: We adore you, O Christ, and we praise you.

All: For by your holy cross, you have redeemed the world.

REFLECTION

Leader: "For we do not have a high priest who is unable to sympathize with our weaknesses, but we have one who in every respect has been tested as we are, yet without sin. Let us therefore approach the throne of grace with boldness, so that we may receive mercy and find grace to help in time of need" (Hebrews 4:15–16). Jesus is now on his journey to Calvary. In stumbling and falling he identifies with our difficulties in reaching our destiny. He does not sin, but he patiently deals with our sinfulness and offers his weaknesses for our salvation. As Son of God he had no power to die. He had to take from us our mortal flesh. Of ourselves, we had no power to gain eternal life. As St. Augustine says: "In a wonderful exchange with us through mutual sharing, we gave him the power to die. He gave us the power to live."[1]

All: I hear that modern writers believe that our destination is not as important as the journey. That is a half-truth. My final goal in life is life and joy with God in heaven. From my life experience, I know that the journey is determined by the goal. Athletes know their goal and practice discipline to get there. Every journey has potholes, both physical and moral challenges. As St. Paul reminds me: "So I do not run aimlessly, nor do I box as though beating the air; but I punish my body and enslave it, so that after proclaiming to others I myself should not be disqualified" (1 Corinthians 9:26–27) and "I can do all things through him who strengthens me" (Philippians 4:13). I won't forget that Jesus arose after each fall. He is my secret power to do so.

SCRIPTURE TO PONDER

All: In the days of his flesh, Jesus offered up prayers and supplications, with loud cries and tears, to the one who was able to save him from death, and he was heard because of his reverent submission. (Hebrews 5:7)

PRAYER TO MEET THE CHALLENGE OF THE CROSS

Leader: Let us pray to meet the challenge of the cross.

All: Lord, keep my eyes on the prize—eternal life with you. Jesus, stop me from leading an aimless life.

Leader: Let us respond to each petition with "Lord, hear my prayer."

- For the gift of living a purposeful life, I pray, *"Lord, hear my prayer."*
- For the inner power of Christ's grace, I pray, *"Lord, hear my prayer."*
- For the grace to get up every time I fall, I pray, *"Lord, hear my prayer."*
- For the courage to ask for help in my time of need, I pray, *"Lord, hear my prayer."*

CLOSING PRAYER

All: Jesus, I know that, Son of God though you were, you learned obedience from what you suffered. I struggle with obedience to God's will and pray with all my heart that I learn the lesson you teach me and that I receive from you the gift of eternal life. Obedience is tough. You can make it possible for me. Thank you, Jesus. Amen.

Leader: We adore you, O Christ, and we praise you.

All: For by your holy cross, you have redeemed the world.

REFLECTION

Leader: In church history Mary is our honored intercessor for divine favors. We should remember that between Mary and her Son there existed a bond between the incredible mother, who was both a believer and a disciple, and her exceptionally devoted son. At Cana, Mary released her Son for his mission: "Do whatever he tells you" (John 2:5). Now she sees the reality prophesied by Simeon. The sword pierces her maternal heart. For thirty years in Nazareth, Mary contemplated the mystery of her beloved Jesus. Her deep silences accompanied her training. Its fulfillment stands before her now. Only love could accept what faith tells her about her suffering son. Jesus pauses to greet his mother in silent communion. Our Lady of Mercy engages her beloved Son of Mercy.

All: Mother Mary reminds me of my need for family support in times of suffering and loss. In such trying times I reach out to family and friends to help me get through the experience.

I stop to think of all those whom I want to forgive, and I ponder how much I want to be forgiven once more for wounds I have inflicted. When I envision this scene when Mary and Jesus exchange glances of forgiveness to those who created their sorrow, I see too that neither Mary nor Jesus shows the least sign of resentment or bitterness. Both display mercy as the true road to the future, my future. Mercy is just what I want and need to give others. I fix my eyes on the serene patience of Jesus and Mary.

SCRIPTURE TO PONDER

All: I will bless the LORD at all times;
   his praise shall continually be in my mouth….
I sought the LORD, and he answered me,
   and delivered me from all my fears….
The LORD is near to the brokenhearted,
   and saves the crushed in spirit.
(Psalm 34:1, 4, 18)

PRAYER TO MEET THE CHALLENGE OF THE CROSS

Leader: Let us pray to meet the challenge of the cross.

All: Lord, don't let your love grow cold in me because of hurts I feel. Jesus, help me give true love to those who harmed me.

Leader: Let us respond to each petition with "Lord, hear my prayer."

- For the times I struggle in my relationships, I pray, *"Lord, hear my prayer."*
- For the healing of relationships in my family, I pray, *"Lord, hear my prayer."*
- For the growth of community where I live, I pray, *"Lord, hear my prayer."*
- For the purity of my intentions, I pray, *"Lord, hear my prayer."*

CLOSING PRAYER

All: Mother Mary, help me to resist the promptings of my sinful nature. Jesus, help me to exhibit maturity in my attitude to others. Through meditating on the gentleness of your humanity, may I expand my capacity to love. Amen.

FIFTH STATION
**SIMON OF CYRENE
HELPS JESUS**

Leader: We adore you, O Christ, and we praise you.

All: For by your holy cross, you have redeemed the world.

REFLECTION

Leader: Fearing that Christ's loss of blood caused by the scourgings and crowning with thorns might kill him before the crucifixion, the soldiers forced Simon to carry the cross (Matthew 27:32). Simon would be the first man to carry the cross of Jesus, who had taught, "Take my yoke upon you, and learn from me; …For my yoke is easy, and my burden is light" (Matthew 11:29–30). While Simon was reluctant, he was a caregiver for Christ, a gift that could bring him to be a disciple. He would never have heard Christ's words, but he carried the burden of the Word made flesh. So close to the Savior, Simon walked in the path of salvation.

All: I have known times when I have been asked to give care to a loved one, a neighbor, a coworker, a stranger. This role of caregiver can drain me in many ways—straining my finances, patience, time, and energy. I find sometimes that I want to say "no" when asked to give care, but soon I say "yes" and get on with doing what is needed. At these times, I try to see the image of Simon, who said "no" but then carried the cross of Jesus and was blessed by God's Son. Simon made it possible for Jesus to accomplish the final act of salvation at Calvary, and I want to have that same privilege. Like Simon, Blessed Mother Teresa of Calcutta and her nuns are an outstanding witness to me of how to give care with kindness and humility.

SCRIPTURE TO PONDER

All: Bear one another's burdens, and in this way you will fulfill the law of Christ. (Galatians 6:2)

PRAYER TO MEET THE CHALLENGE OF THE CROSS

Leader: Let us pray to meet the challenge of the cross.

All: Lord, give me the courage to be a caregiver. Jesus, show me the wisdom of the cross in being a caregiver.

Leader: Let us respond to each petition with "Lord, hear my prayer."

- For dealing with my elderly relatives, friends, and neighbors, I pray, *"Lord, hear my prayer."*

- For those who nurse the poor and the neglected, I pray, *"Lord, hear my prayer."*
- For those in hospice care, I pray, *"Lord, hear my prayer."*
- For my acceptance of Christ's yoke and burden, I pray, *"Lord, hear my prayer."*

CLOSING PRAYER

All: Lord, I pray for the graces I need to serve the poor, the hungry, the naked, the sick, the elderly, the dying. Open me to accept the challenges of the cross you wish me to carry. Forgive me for my reluctance to bear your cross. Grant me the joy that comes from loving service to you in the needs of others. Amen.

Leader: We adore you, O Christ, and we praise you.

All: For by your holy cross, you have redeemed the world.

REFLECTION

Leader: Veronica is a legendary woman who was moved with compassion for the sufferings of Jesus, especially for the blood and sweat that marred his face. While the incident is not mentioned in the Gospels, her story emerged in early writings about the Passion. She wiped Jesus' face with a cloth on which his image was imprinted. It is noted that her name comes from the Latin words *vera* ("true") and *icon* ("picture"). The holy veil is kept today in St. Peter's Basilica in Vatican City. It recalls the words of Isaiah that found fulfillment in Jesus: "I gave my back to those who struck me, / and my cheeks to those who pulled out the beard; / I did not hide my face / from insult and spitting" (Isaiah 50:6).

All: I have witnessed—and perhaps experienced —the physical sufferings that require medical care, and the dependence that causes someone to hold a comforting cloth to a brow or provide a compassionate touch. My vanity and pride often make me resent such dependency.

Bl. John Paul II, frail in his later years, wore his cross publicly. When asked if he intended to resign the papacy, he replied, "Did Jesus come down from the cross?" The wounds to my pride sometimes are worse than the ones to my body. Jesus looked awful on the way to Calvary, yet he paused and let a kindly woman clear his face. He rewarded her with an imprint, but more so with gratitude. I see Veronica's gesture and Jesus' response as an invitation for me to cherish the singular blessings of humility.

SCRIPTURE TO PONDER

All: Therefore I am content with weaknesses, insults, hardships, persecutions, and calamities for the sake of Christ; for whenever I am weak, then I am strong. (2 Corinthians 12:10)

PRAYER TO MEET THE CHALLENGE OF THE CROSS

Leader: Let us pray to meet the challenge of the cross.

All: Lord, restrain my discomfort in depending on the care of others when I am ill. Encourage me to welcome your calls to humility.

Leader: Let us respond to each petition with "Lord, hear my prayer."

- For humility on my way of the cross, I pray, *"Lord, hear my prayer."*
- For the gift of gratitude to my caregivers when I am ill, I pray, *"Lord, hear my prayer."*
- For the grace to imitate Christ's Passion, I pray, *"Lord, hear my prayer."*
- For a deeper faith and love for Christ, I pray, *"Lord, hear my prayer."*

CLOSING PRAYER

All: Lord, help me to see the value of my own way of the cross when I unite it with Christ's Passion. Show me how the problem of pain and suffering is a door to the purification of my soul. Teach me the meaning of the words of Jesus, who said that being his disciple involves self-denial and bearing the cross, and so I will be able to follow him. Help me to realize this is the best way to make sense of suffering. Amen.

Leader: We adore you, O Christ, and we praise you.

All: For by your holy cross, you have redeemed the world.

REFLECTION

Leader: The physical assaults on Christ's body led to his falls on the way to Calvary. With the eyes of faith we understand that his falls are part of his self-emptying as described in Scripture: "who, though he was in the form of God, / did not regard equality with God / as something to be exploited, / but emptied himself, / taking the form of a slave, / being born in human likeness. / And being found in human form, / he humbled himself / and became obedient to the point of death— / even death on a cross" (Philippians 2:6–8). Jesus' falls forecast his death, but his rising hinted at his victory over death itself on the third day. Knowing of Jesus' divinity, I am slow to recognize Jesus' humility in becoming human, to see him in the midst of his self-emptying. In our natural world, what goes up must come down. In our supernatural world, what goes down should go up.

All: Jesus fell and got up for me. I know love made him do this. Infinite love will do the unthinkable. Meditations about the Passion of Christ dramatize Jesus on the ground, weighed down by torture as well as by the burden of my sinfulness. He took a human nature so that he could know human life from the inside and have the capacity to endure human suffering. In so doing he was able to provide me with a path out of my sinfulness and a way to deal with the pitfalls and tragedies of my everyday life. When I tire of being beaten into the ground, I know that Jesus wants to give me the strength to get up again. That's why he experienced falls—so that he could win for me my risings to carry on with my life. The dust from the Jerusalem street was on his face. But his affection for me stirred in his heart so that I too could get up once more with hope and confidence.

SCRIPTURE TO PONDER

All: For while we live, we are always being given up to death for Jesus' sake, so that the life of Jesus may be made visible in our mortal flesh. (2 Corinthians 4:11)

PRAYER TO MEET THE CHALLENGE OF THE CROSS

Leader: Let us pray to meet the challenge of the cross.

All: Lord, give me the strength to get up again after the setbacks in my life. Share with me the courage you had to rise again after each fall on the road to Calvary.

Leader: Let us respond to each petition with "Lord, hear my prayer."

- For the courage to rise again after difficulties, I pray, *"Lord, hear my prayer."*
- For the wisdom to expect trials in my life, I pray, *"Lord, hear my prayer."*
- For the faith I seek in the face of suffering, I pray, *"Lord, hear my prayer."*
- In thanksgiving for Christ rising after his falls, I pray, *"Lord, hear my prayer."*

CLOSING PRAYER

All: Lord, increase my awareness of the role of setbacks on my journey of faith. Show me the values you witnessed by your constant self-emptying, especially during the drama of your passage to the cross. May I see in your falls your willingness to endure more self-emptying, even to the end of life. Open my eyes of faith and help me to identify the love that made it possible for you to rise after every fall. Amen.

EIGHTH STATION
JESUS SPEAKS TO THE DAUGHTERS OF JERUSALEM

Leader: We adore you, O Christ, and we praise you.

All: For by your holy cross, you have redeemed the world.

REFLECTION

Leader: Jesus did not walk alone: "A great number of the people followed him, and among them were women who were beating their breasts and wailing for him. But Jesus turned to them and said, 'Daughters of Jerusalem, do not weep for me, but weep for yourselves and for your children'" (Luke 23:27–28). As always, Jesus thinks of others before his own needs. He worries about the future of these women and their children. He is telling them that productive life depends on the well-being of women. They will not flourish if culture fails to appreciate their essential role as wives, mothers, or virginal mentors. If a culture belittles women's responsibility to the next generation, everyone is endangered.

All: In this remarkable scene, I witness Jesus halting his journey briefly to stand up for the needs of women—not only in that culture but today as well. I am concerned and at times alarmed by the collapse of marriages, the rising number of single-parent homes, the poverty that sometimes is a result, and the harm to children that is widespread in the advanced culture of the West. I see Jesus weeping for so many of today's women and children who need my support to ensure strong family values, economic stability, and a promising future. On the road to Calvary, Jesus pauses to explain one reason he is saving the world—and me: He is obtaining for me the graces I—and mothers and children—need to thrive spiritually and physically.

SCRIPTURE TO PONDER

All: I now am taking this kinswoman of mine,
   not because of lust,
   but with sincerity.
Grant that she and I may find mercy
   and that we may grow old together. (Tobit 8:7)

PRAYER TO MEET THE CHALLENGE OF THE CROSS

Leader: Let us pray to meet the challenge of the cross.

All: Lord, give me the strength, grace, and freedom to support women and children, marriage and family life.

Leader: Let us respond to each petition with "Lord, hear my prayer."

- For the graces I need to support family life, *"Lord, hear my prayer."*
- For a culture that promotes family values, *"Lord, hear my prayer."*
- For a recovery of stable marriages, *"Lord, hear my prayer."*
- For respect for the dignity of women, *"Lord, hear my prayer."*

CLOSING PRAYER

All: Lord, thank you for taking time in the midst of your own pain to speak to the special needs of the women of Jerusalem and their children. Women stayed the course and witnessed your death on the cross. You honored women with the first revelations of your resurrection from the dead and commissioned them to announce the good news to the apostles. I pray for a renewed commitment to the essential role of women, along with that of men, for a responsible future for marriage and the family in our culture. Amen.

Leader: We adore you, O Christ, and we praise you.

All: For by your holy cross, you have redeemed the world.

REFLECTION

Leader: When St. Paul walked his way of the cross, he learned from Christ about how to handle obstacles while finishing the quest. "We also boast in our sufferings, knowing that suffering produces endurance, and endurance produces character, and character produces hope" (Romans 5:3–4). Paul did endure, as he later wrote, "I have fought the good fight, I have finished the race, I have kept the faith" (2 Timothy 4:7). In his third fall Jesus faced what athletes might call a "wall," and he persevered through the final steps to the cross. In heading for his destiny, Jesus encountered a devastating fall that challenged him to rise and move on. He did this for us, fulfilling Isaiah's words: "Surely he has borne our infirmities / and carried our diseases" (Isaiah 53:4).

All: I remember Christ's last thrust to Calvary when the apostle James wrote, "My brothers and sisters, whenever you face trials of any kind, consider it nothing but joy, because you know that the testing of your faith produces endurance" (James 1:2–3). I tend to focus on the pain and find it difficult to notice the joy that James mentions. I pray that I may imitate the attitude of Peter and his companions, who faced persecution joyfully for proclaiming Christ. Having just been flogged, "as they left the council, they rejoiced that they were considered worthy to suffer dishonor for the sake of the name [of Jesus]" (Acts 5:41). At the same time, I must admit it will not be easy. I agree with the challenge of St. Gregory of Nyssa: "We must sacrifice ourselves to God, each day and in everything we do, accepting all that happens to us for the sake of the Word, imitating his passion by our sufferings, and honoring his blood by shedding our own. We must be ready to be crucified."[1]

SCRIPTURE TO PONDER

All: Draw near to God, and he will draw near to you.… Humble yourselves before the Lord, and he will exalt you. (James 4:8, 10)

PRAYER TO MEET THE CHALLENGE OF THE CROSS

Leader: Let us pray to meet the challenge of the cross.

All: Lord, stand by me when I reach a roadblock

and I have no strength to break through it. I need your spiritual power.

Leader: Let us respond to each petition with "Lord, hear my prayer."

- For the spiritual resources I need to keep going, *"Lord, hear my prayer."*
- For confidence in Christ who strengthens me, *"Lord, hear my prayer."*
- For the trust I seek in Christ's promises, *"Lord, hear my prayer."*
- For the gift of hope, *"Lord, hear my prayer."*

CLOSING PRAYER

All: Lord, I praise you for your example of courage in your darkest hour on the road to the cross. I love you for winning for me the spiritual power to face my own demons and move beyond them because of your gift to me. I am learning to trust you, and I realize more and more how profound is your all-embracing love for me and all the world. Amen.

---

1. *Liturgy of the Hours,* vol. 2 (New York: Catholic Book, 1988), p. 393.

Leader: We adore you, O Christ, and we praise you.

All: For by your holy cross, you have redeemed the world.

REFLECTION

Leader: In his Last Judgment sermon, Jesus said, "I was naked and you gave me clothing" (Matthew 25:36). At Calvary the soldiers stripped Jesus of his clothing. Jesus had praised the poor in spirit, and now he identified with the poorest of the poor who barely have anything to wear. His self-emptying reached yet another level as human beings tried to rob him of his last shred of dignity. The wisdom of St. Athanasius applies to Christ's Passion when he said that the unassumed is the unhealed. At Calvary Jesus witnessed that the crucified is the healed. He lets down the walls that might protect him. He is vulnerable, a word taken from the Latin *vulnus,* meaning "wound." Our lifetime of regrets and unfinished business lingers in our memories. His way of the cross is a catalog of wounds on our behalf.

All: Why does Jesus allow himself to be so vulnerable? Because he intends to heal the hurters. When I am vulnerable and wounded,

I often strike back with insults, betrayals, and slights. When I hurt Christ, he forgets the wounds and tries to heal me, the hurter. To Jesus the real wound is in the one inflicting the pain. Jesus assumes the difficulties of the hurter and offers healing by the therapy of forgiveness and love. While the hurter tries to strip Jesus of his dignity, he offers a path to rediscover the dignity lost through brutal behavior. Jesus welcomes me as a sinner into the chambers of his heart and lets me thrash about with my unruly passions. Then he offers me the love that would cure me of my irrational evil. Isaiah illustrated this truth with these words that were realized by Christ: "By his bruises we are healed. / He was oppressed, and he was afflicted, / yet he did not open his mouth; / like a lamb that is led to the slaughter, / and like a sheep that before its shearers is silent" (Isaiah 53:5, 7). I know that Jesus was not completely silent, that he spoke a few words: "Father, forgive them; for they do not know what they are doing" (Luke 23:34).

SCRIPTURE TO PONDER

All: For the message about the cross is foolishness to those who are perishing, but to us who are being saved it is the power of God. (1 Corinthians 1:18)

PRAYER TO MEET THE CHALLENGE OF THE CROSS

Leader: Let us pray to meet the challenge of the cross.

All: Lord, teach us the wisdom you witnessed as a wounded healer.

Leader: Let us respond to each petition with "Lord, hear my prayer."

- For the gift of healing those who hurt me, *"Lord, hear my prayer."*
- For the wisdom to love my enemies, *"Lord, hear my prayer."*
- For courage to not strike back when I am wounded, *"Lord, hear my prayer."*
- For forgiveness of my sins, *"Lord, hear my prayer."*

CLOSING PRAYER

All: Lord, engrave on my heart the promise of happiness so I may live the words of Jesus, "Blessed are you when they insult you and persecute you and utter every kind of evil against you falsely on my account. Rejoice and be glad, for your reward is great in heaven" (Matthew 5:11–12). Give me the faith and courage to witness this application of the cross in my life. Amen.

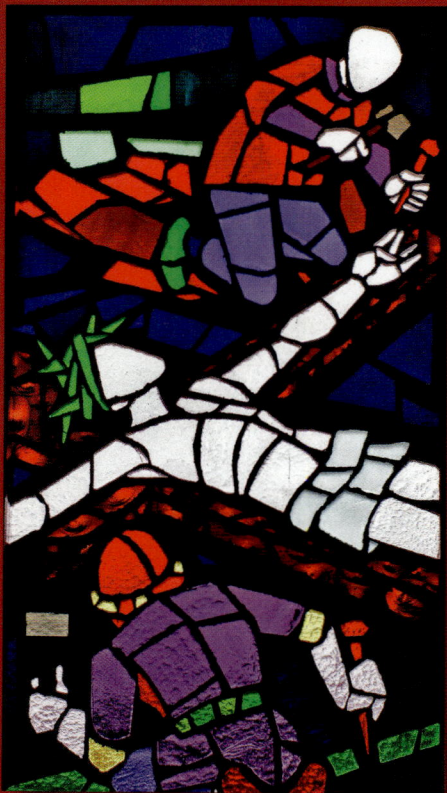

Leader: We adore you, O Christ, and we praise you.

All: For by your holy cross, you have redeemed the world.

REFLECTION

Leader: To think of the pain caused by the nails in Christ's hands and feet is almost too much to bear. Yet we are fascinated to behold the risen Jesus displaying the scars of the nails on his glorified body. The apostle Thomas claimed he would not believe Christ was risen unless he could touch Jesus' scars. So Jesus appeared to Thomas and invited him to do so. A chastened Thomas knelt before Jesus, saying, "My Lord and my God" (John 20:28). The message of the cross is a dominant theme throughout Christian history. Poor, sick, oppressed, and crushed people find comfort in the Passion of Christ. The "man of sorrows" means a great deal to those in pain, especially those among us in nursing homes, hospitals, and hospices, where the love and mercy of the crucified seems near and sympathetic.

All: I hear and sing of the Passion of Jesus in the spirituals of the African slaves. The pain of Christ symbolized the slaves' own sufferings.

Jesus could understand their despised condition in an unfriendly and inhuman world. As far as the slaves were concerned, when the Roman soldier stabbed Christ in the side, he was not alone. They were there with Jesus. The slaves sang, "Were you there when they crucified my Lord?" They sang their own reply, "Oh, sometimes it causes me to tremble, tremble, tremble." In my contemporary world I am called to adore a crucified God and not dilute the cross by smothering it with roses or pleasant thoughts, making its meaning and value vanish. I need the shadows of Good Friday to appreciate the full possibilities of the Easter mystery. The most distant object I can see on a clear day is the sun. But on a dark night I can see the stars, millions of miles farther away. Darkness has its spiritual value. I think of that in my own times of trouble, when I tremble, tremble, tremble.

SCRIPTURE TO PONDER
All: I live by faith in the Son of God, who loved me and gave himself up for me. (Galatians 2:20)

PRAYER TO MEET THE CHALLENGE OF THE CROSS

Leader: Let us pray to meet the challenge of the cross.

All: Lord, deepen my faith in the power of the cross in my life.

Leader: Let us respond to each petition with "Lord, hear my prayer."

- For faith to see the link between Good Friday and Easter, *"Lord, hear my prayer."*
- For recourse to the crucified Christ when I am ill, *"Lord, hear my prayer."*
- For sympathy and care for the oppressed, *"Lord, hear my prayer."*
- For patience in times of personal pain, *"Lord, hear my prayer."*

CLOSING PRAYER

All: Must Jesus bear the Cross alone
   And all the world go free
   No, there's a Cross for everyone
   And there's a Cross for me.

   —from "Amazing Grace," by John Newton, 1779

Leader: We adore you, O Christ, and we praise you.

All: For by your holy cross, you have redeemed the world.

Leader: As the ninth hour approached on Good Friday afternoon, the sacrifice of the Passover lambs at the Temple concluded. The high priest in Hebrew said, *"Kalah"* ("It is finished."). At that moment, Jesus the Lamb of God, said, *"Kalah"* ("It is finished") (John 19:30a). Jesus bowed his head and rested it on the cross. A great silence enfolded that moment, the silence of the Lamb of God. In his death Jesus completed the perfect sacrifice needed for the forgiveness of all the sins of those who repent and seek his divine mercy. John's Gospel describes the last breath of Jesus as the giving of his spirit: "Then he bowed his head and gave up his spirit" (John 19:30b). In a symbolic way Jesus is already giving his Holy Spirit to the faithful ones who stood by his cross—his mother who represented the church and John who stands for the Christian. On Easter night Jesus will make his first appearance to the apostles, when he will breathe the Holy Spirit on them for the forgiveness of sins (John 20:22–23).

All: When I think of Christ's death, I linger on my own future death. I will not be able to choose the time and place of my death, but I can choose my way of life. I hear more clearly the wisdom of people of faith reminding me, "As you live, so shall you die." My death will ratify the kind of life I have lived and the choices I have made. If I have lived with love, that is how I shall die. If not, that will be a tragedy. As he was dying, Jesus gave his life calmly and lovingly to God, for that was how he lived. He didn't leave any money. He left an incomparable testament: divine mercy, future life, and sustaining hope. His deathbed provided the most profound lesson in dying the world has ever seen and will ever see. With this in mind, I pray that my last moments, my dying, will be filled with the same grace.

SCRIPTURE TO PONDER

All: For to this you have been called, because Christ also suffered for you, leaving you an example, so that you should follow in his steps.… When he was abused, he did not return abuse; when he suffered, he did not threaten;… He himself bore our sins in his body on the cross, so that, free from sins, we might live for righteousness; by his wounds you have been healed. (1 Peter 2:21, 23–24)

PRAYER TO MEET THE CHALLENGE OF THE CROSS

Leader: Let us pray to meet the challenge of the cross.

All: Lord, unite me to your way of facing death.

Leader: Let us respond to each petition with "Lord, hear my prayer."

- For the gift of dying in the peace of Christ, *"Lord, hear my prayer."*
- For the blessings of living in the graces of God, *"Lord, hear my prayer."*
- For faith in life after death, *"Lord, hear my prayer."*
- For faith in the resurrection of my body, *"Lord, hear my prayer."*

CLOSING PRAYER

All: Hold thou thy cross before my closing eyes; shine through the gloom and point me to the skies.

Heaven's morning breaks, and earth's vain shadows flee;

in life, in death, O Lord, abide with me.

—from "Abide With Me," by Henry Francis Lyte, 1847

JESUS IS TAKEN DOWN FROM THE CROSS

Leader: We adore you, O Christ, and we praise you.

All: For by your holy cross, you have redeemed the world.

REFLECTION

Leader: Christian faith and imagination tends to fill in what Scripture omits. Such is the case with the scene of Jesus taken down from the cross and placed in the arms of Mary, his mother. Michelangelo's sculpture, the *Pietà*, which in Italian means "pity," supplies that scene. Other sculptors had created the scene, but none with the power of Michelangelo. He placed a grown man in a woman's lap. He portrayed none of the violence of the Passion. The nail holes in Christ's hands and feet are tiny. Bathed in tranquillity, Jesus and Mary glow with light because the marble is polished to velvet silkiness. Draped peacefully in his mother's arms, Jesus reveals a silent composure that in itself communicates a sense of the divine. Michelangelo produced a harmony between mother and son that spoke of God's new and harmonious relationship with the world. The sculptor was asked why he made Mary's face so young, younger than her son. He replied that it seemed to him that the Virgin

Mary would not age, because she was pure and she would have kept the freshness of youth.[1]

All: Bl. John XXIII was fond of quoting an old Italian proverb, *"Sotto la neve c'e il pane"* ("Beneath the snow there is bread."). Rural wisdom remembers that the seed under the winter snow will rise in the springtime. Bl. John XXIII applied the saying to those overwhelmed by sorrow and unable to see beyond the pain. Using his picture, I see the snow. I do not see the bread of love growing quietly underneath that white blanket. While countless mothers have held their dead sons in their arms and mourned desperately their loss, my faith tells me that at death, life is changed, not taken away. I carry the seed of eternity in my immortal soul. Like Mary, who was profoundly saddened by her son's death, I mourn Jesus yet believe in his promise of resurrection.

SCRIPTURE TO PONDER

All: For I know that my Redeemer lives, and that at the last he will stand upon the earth;…then in my flesh I shall see God. (Job 19:25–26b)

PRAYER TO MEET THE CHALLENGE OF THE CROSS

Leader: Let us pray to meet the challenge of the cross.

All: Lord, increase my faith in life after death.

Leader: Let us respond to each petition with "Lord, hear my prayer."

- For a deeper faith in life after death, *"Lord, hear my prayer."*
- For the gift of consoling those who mourn lost ones, *"Lord, hear my prayer."*
- For respect for the bodies of the deceased, *"Lord, hear my prayer."*
- For the protection of preborn life, *"Lord, hear my prayer."*

CLOSING PRAYER

All: Lord, help me to pray seriously the words of our Creed: "I believe in the resurrection of the body and life everlasting." Show me how to support life from conception to natural death. Console me when I will need to grieve the death of a loved one while I retain belief in eternal life. Amen.

1. This paragraph has been adapted from my book *The Seven Last Words of Jesus* (Cincinnati: St. Anthony Messenger Press, 1990), pp. 82–83. The original source for my work was the novel based on the life of Michelangelo by Irving Stone, *The Agony and the Ecstasy* (New York: Doubleday, 1961).

Leader: We adore you, O, Christ, and we praise you.

All: For by your holy cross, you have redeemed the world.

REFLECTION

Leader: Jesus once said it would be harder for a rich man to get to heaven than for a camel to go through the eye of a needle. Now two wealthy men come to bury Jesus. Joseph of Arimathea obtained from Pilate permission to bury the body of Jesus. Taking the body, Joseph laid it in his new tomb (cf. Matthew 27:57–60). Meanwhile, "Nicodemus…also came, bringing a mixture of myrrh and aloes, weighing about a hundred pounds. They took the body of Jesus and wrapped it with the spices in linen cloths" (John 19:39–40). Then they rolled a huge stone against the door of the tomb and departed. These two men were the first to fulfill the saying of Jesus: "And I, when I am lifted up from the earth, will draw all people to myself" (John 12:32). The little party of mourners besides the men were Christ's mother, Mary Magdalene, and two other women. Before closing the tomb they recited the traditional funeral prayer, "Dust you are and unto dust you will return." They were going to be surprised!

All: I find the rites of Christian burial to be essential ways of surrounding the loved one with a spirit of faith, a belief in the future life, and a way to grieve with a believing community. I love the Mass of Christian Burial, which renews for us the sacrificial banquet of Christ, providing the Bread of Life for our souls and a promise of salvation for the beloved. I am moved by the Song of Farewell as the body is taken for burial. I am saddened when some families fail to provide these rites, especially for parents and grandparents who expect this gift. The white pall that covers the coffin recalls baptism and symbolizes the promise of resurrection. These signs of faith link me solidly to the afterlife of the beloved. I pray for fidelity to this liturgy and the family rituals that are expected.

SCRIPTURE TO PONDER

All: When Mary came where Jesus was and saw him, she knelt at his feet and said to him, "Lord, if you had been here, my brother would not have died." When Jesus saw her weeping, and the Jews who had come with her also weeping, he was greatly disturbed in spirit and deeply moved. (John 11:32–33)

PRAYER TO MEET THE CHALLENGE OF THE CROSS

Leader: Let us pray to meet the challenge of the cross.

All: Lord, abide with us when we mourn our loved ones.

Leader: Let us respond to each petition with "Lord, hear my prayer."

- For the graces found in the rites of Christian burial, *"Lord, hear my prayer."*
- For the ability to mourn in a spirit of faith, *"Lord, hear my prayer."*
- For the grace to console those who mourn, *"Lord, hear my prayer."*
- For respect for the remains of loved ones and all who have died, *"Lord, hear my prayer."*

CLOSING PRAYER

All: Blessed be the God and Father of our Lord Jesus Christ, the Father of mercies and the God of all consolation, who consoles us in all our affliction, so that to those who are in any affliction we may be able to offer the consolation with which we ourselves are consoled by God. Amen. (2 Corinthians 1:3–4)

Leader: We adore you, O Christ, and we praise you.

All: For by your holy cross, you have redeemed the world.

REFLECTION

Leader: We need to approach the mystery of Christ's resurrection with a faith enveloped in love. We are dealing with the mysterious link between knowledge and love. St. Augustine tells us, "Give me a lover and he will understand." What are some of the events our love sees at Easter? The Emmaus disciples perceive Jesus in the breaking of the bread. At our Easter Masses we adore our Risen Lord. We hear the Gospel stories of the number of times Jesus appears to the disciples when they gather for shared prayer or meals. John's Gospel connects the resurrection with forgiveness of sins. On Easter night Jesus confers the Holy Spirit on the apostles and imparts to them the ministry of reconciliation (John 20:22–23). Who can forget the Easter scene by the lake where Peter makes a triple confession of love of Jesus to repair his three denials?

All: When I read or listen to the resurrection narratives, I see that, though glorified now, Jesus has not lost his humanity. He took the hands of the disciples and urged them to touch him, embrace him, and feel his bones and flesh. He was no ghost. While he now manifests his divine glory as the Word, he is still the Word made flesh. Even though the disciples now believed in Jesus' resurrection, their faith, like mine, still needed strengthening. Easter faith is a growth process, a growing in faith to see and believe the essential truths about how Jesus has saved me from sin and offered me divine life. I sing with joy the Easter hymn: "The strife is o'er, the battle done, / the victory of life is won; / the song of triumph has begun. / Alleluia!

SCRIPTURE TO PONDER

All: For the trumpet will sound, and the dead will be raised imperishable, and we will be changed…thanks be to God, who gives us the victory through our Lord Jesus Christ. (1 Corinthians 15:52, 57)

PRAYER TO MEET THE CHALLENGE OF THE CROSS

Leader: Let us pray to meet the challenge of the cross.

All: Risen Lord, show us the how the cross leads to resurrection.

Leader: Let us respond to each petition with "Lord, hear my prayer."

- For joy in anticipation of my resurrection, *"Lord, hear my prayer."*
- In thanksgiving for the resurrection of Christ, *"Lord, hear my prayer."*
- For faith in Christ's risen presence in the Eucharist, *"Lord, hear my prayer."*
- For a sense of new life for me in Christ, *"Lord, hear my prayer."*

CLOSING PRAYER

All: O God, do not forsake me,
until I proclaim your might
        to all the generations to come.
Your power and your righteousness, O God,
        reach the high heavens.

...

You will increase my honor,
        and comfort me once again.

I will also praise you with the harp
    for your faithfulness, O my God;
I will sing praises to you with the lyre,
    O Holy One of Israel.
My lips will shout for joy
    when I sing praises to you;
      my soul also, which you have rescued.
All day long my tongue will talk of your
      righteous help.
(Psalm 71:18–19, 21–24)